The Adventures of Scuba Jack
Copyright 2021 by Beth Costanzo
All rights reserved

In our exploration of many of the most fascinating *sea creatures* on the planet, we haven't yet talked about one of the *largest*. This animal is huge and can appear scary when you look at it. However, when you learn more about it, you discover that this animal is beautiful and fascinating.

www.adventuresofscubajack.com

I am talking about the **whale shark**. While you may not see a **whale shark** in the wild or in your aquarium, it is an extremely interesting creature that is worth studying further.

www.adventuresofscubajack.com

The Whale Shark: Some Basic Facts

www.adventuresofscubajack.com

To start, one of the most striking things about **whale sharks** is their *size*. They are the *largest* sharks in the *world*. On average, adult **whale sharks** are *30 feet* (9.1 meters) long, roughly the size of a school bus, and weigh *20,000 pounds* (9,072 kilograms) - as heavy as two elephants!

www.adventuresofscubajack.com

The largest **whale shark** on record was *41.5 feet* (12.6 meters) long and weighed *56,000 pounds* (25,401 kilograms). Now you know how it got its name! Here's a shark that can grow up to the size of a whale. In fact, it is even larger than a lot of whales.

www.adventuresofscubajack.com

Moreover, the **whale shark** is not only the *largest* shark. It is the largest fish in the ocean and the largest backboned animal that isn't a mammal. If you were to see a **whale shark** in the ocean, you would immediately notice how large they are! The good part, though, is that **whale sharks** pose no threat to humans, so you wouldn't need to worry about them trying to attack or feed on you.

www.adventuresofscubajack.com

Beyond their huge size, **whale sharks** are beautiful creatures. They have *pale yellow spots* and *stripes* on their *bluish* skin. These spots and stripes are unique to individual **whale sharks**. This means that the **whale shark** you see appears different than all other whale sharks in the ocean.

The skin of the **whale shark** can be very hard and rough to the touch. It has some massive fins that help it swim throughout the ocean. Finally, **whale sharks** have large, flattened heads, but small eyes about the size of golf balls and barbels (which are like whiskers) around their nostrils.

www.adventuresofscubajack.com

Looking at their history, **whale sharks** have been around our planet for a long time. In fact, some scientists estimate that they have been around for 60 million years. In terms of their lifespan, **whale sharks** typically live for about 70 years. This is close to how long humans normally live! Scientists predict that the oldest whale sharks have lived for around 130 years.

www.adventuresofscubajack.com

Whale sharks live in warm waters all over the world. If you were to try looking for them, you may find them swimming just below the surface. That said, you may need to travel far to find them. **Whale sharks** can be found in open waters of tropical oceans and aren't often found in waters that are lower than *70 degrees Fahrenheit*. People have spotted **whale sharks** near *South Africa*, *Western Australia*, and even *Indonesia*. They are rarely spotted off the shores of the United States.

www.adventuresofscubajack.com

The **whale shark** is a filter feeder, which means that it opens its mouth and sucks in a lot of water. Then it closes its mouth and filters the water out gills so that only the food remains inside. It eats plankton, algae, krill, small squid, and crab larvae. In order to take in a lot of water, a whale shark has to open its mouth really wide. It can open its mouth up to 5 feet (1.5 meters) wide. That's large enough to swallow a whole bathtub! A **whale shark** can filter through more than *1,500 gallons* (*5,678 liters*) of water per *hour*.

www.adventuresofscubajack.com

When a **whale shark** opens its mouth, you will see its numerous teeth. It has even more teeth than the *great white shark* (up to 4,000 teeth arranged in hundreds of rows). These teeth, however, are tiny and not at all sharp like the great white's. Rather, they look like rasps. These little teeth, however, are not used for feeding.

www.adventuresofscubajack.com

Whale sharks are not afraid of boats, ships, fishing vessels, or yachts. Unfortunately, whale sharks often collide with boats and get injured in boat collisions. This is mostly due to their large size (it can be tough to avoid objects and other animals when you're this big!). It isn't because they want to threaten or attack humans.

www.adventuresofscubajack.com

Like other animals in the ocean, **whale sharks** can be eaten by other animals. Because of their size, however, they have fewer predators compared to other animals. For example, **whale shark** pups may be eaten by larger sharks and other large fish (such as blue marlins). The greatest threat to **whale sharks** are humans, who hunt them for their meat and fins. When getting close to humans, **whale sharks** will often swim away due to fear, rather than attack humans or boats.

www.adventuresofscubajack.com

While there are significantly fewer whale sharks today than there were in the past, you can still see them in the wild. Whale sharks are seen in waters near South Africa, the Philippines, and Mexico. These animals like to stay in water that is at least 70 degrees. While they are not known to live near the ocean floor, some whale sharks have been as deep as 5,900 feet.

Whale sharks tend to live much longer than other types of marine life. They have a lifespan of around 80 years, but some whale sharks have lived to up to 130 years old. Female whale sharks give birth to pups that are up to two feet long.

In sum, the whale shark is a large and fascinating creature. Even though there are very few of them left alive today, keep an eye out for them when you are swimming in the ocean!

Some More Fun Facts

The whale shark is one of the most fascinating creatures in our oceans. If you see one in real life, you will be amazed by its beauty and size. It is unlike many other animals out there.

To impress your friends, family, and classmates, here are some more fun facts about the whale shark.

www.adventuresofscubajack.com

A child whale shark is estimated to eat around 46 pounds of plankton per day.

Whale sharks sometimes let swimmers grab onto their fins and catch a ride. That said, scientists discourage this because it may disturb these whale sharks.

www.adventuresofscubajack.com

The whale shark species is considered endangered because of fisheries, vessel strikes, and other threats.

In 2011, 400 whale sharks gathered off of the Yucatan Coast. This was one of the largest ever gatherings of whale sharks recorded in the wild.

www.adventuresofscubajack.com

The whale shark species was discovered in the year 1828.

_____

Large numbers of whale sharks often congregate between May and September.

_____

www.adventuresofscubajack.com

Whale Sharks Activities

www.adventuresofscubajack.com

Trace

Trace the phrase then write it below

W is for Whale Shark

7 differences

Spot the 7 differences

www.adventuresofscubajack.com

Counting

Count the whale sharks and the little fishes and put the correct answer in the box

www.adventuresofscubajack.com

Counting

Count the number of White-Sharks and Whale-Sharks below:

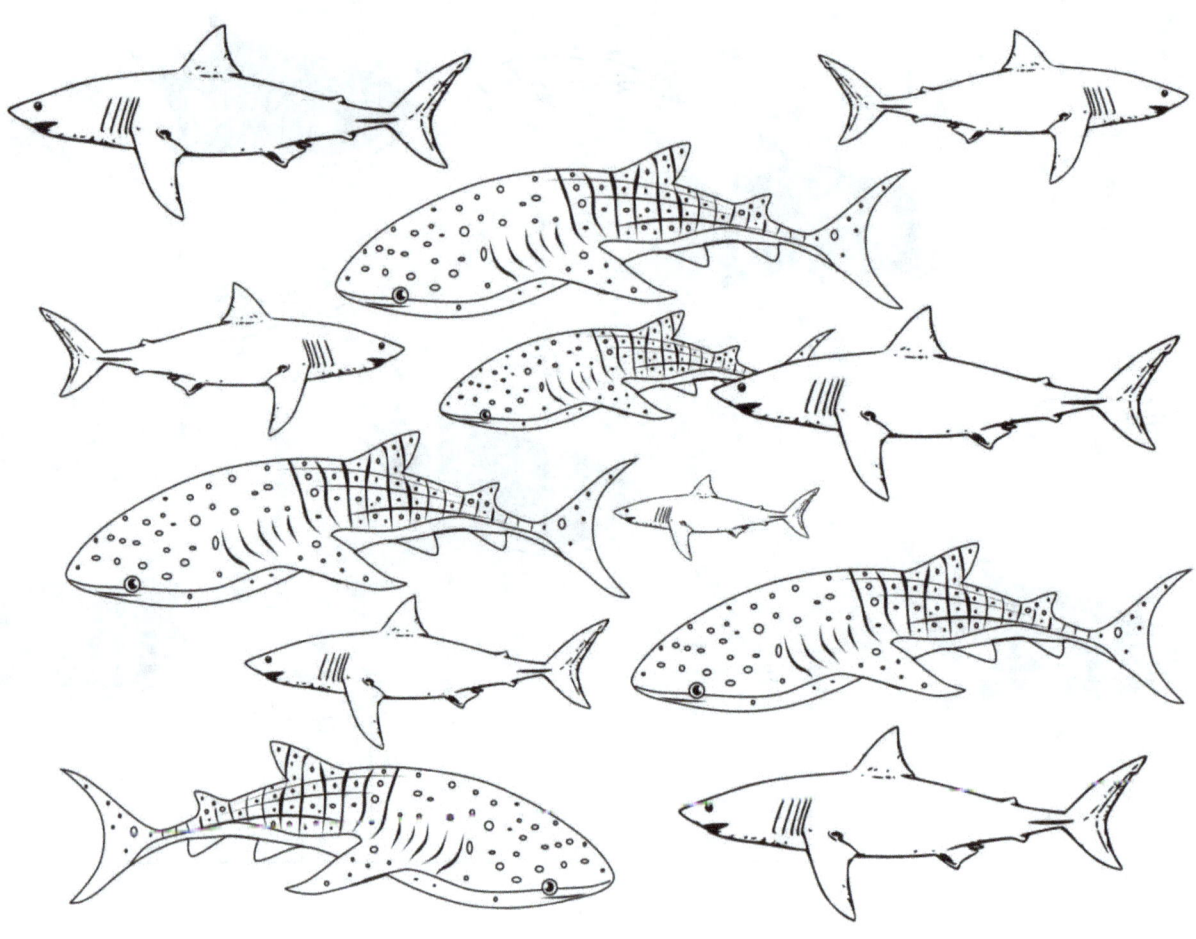

Number of White-Sharks is: ☐

Number of Whale-Sharks is: ☐

www.adventuresofscubajack.com

Coloring

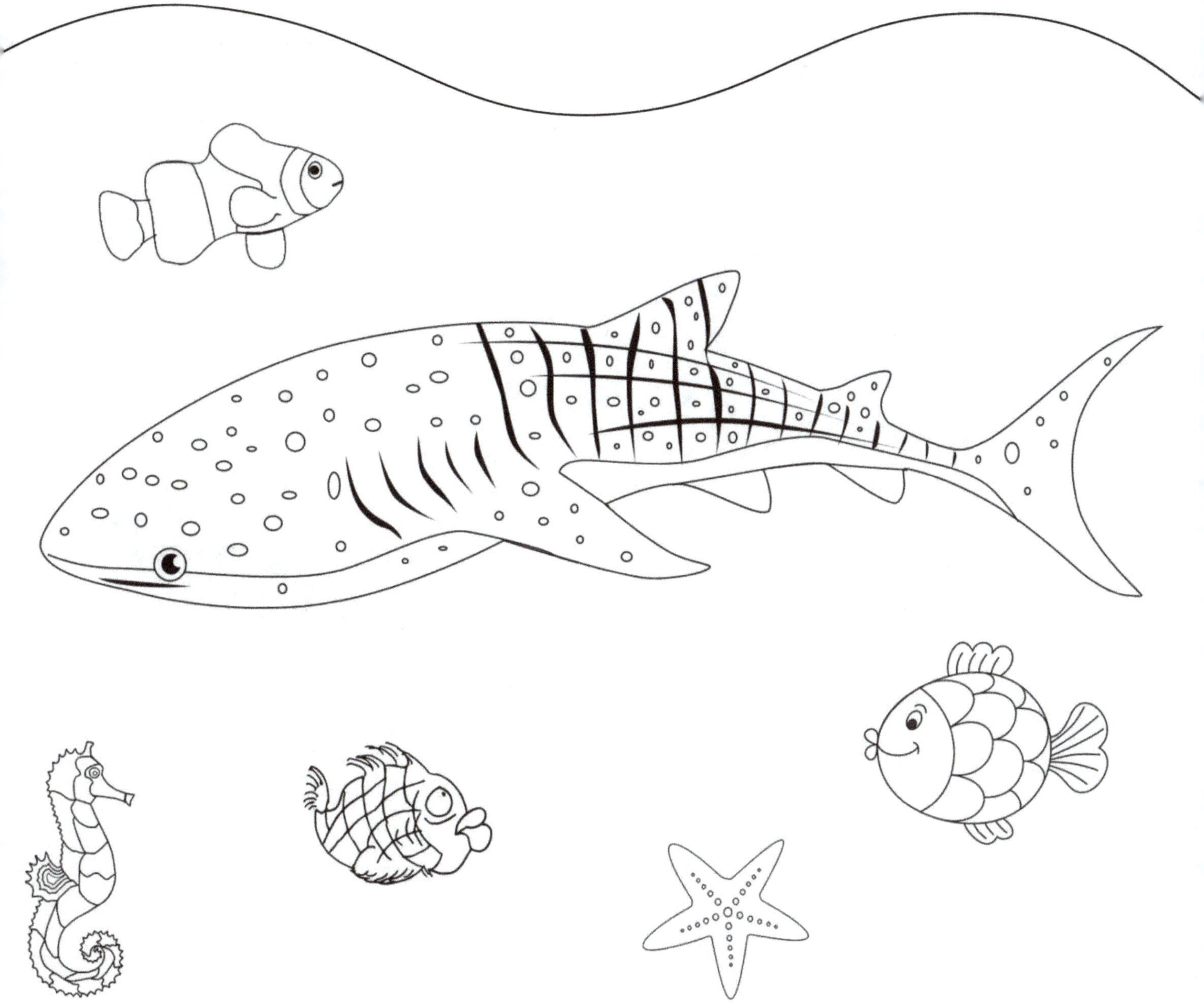

Coloring

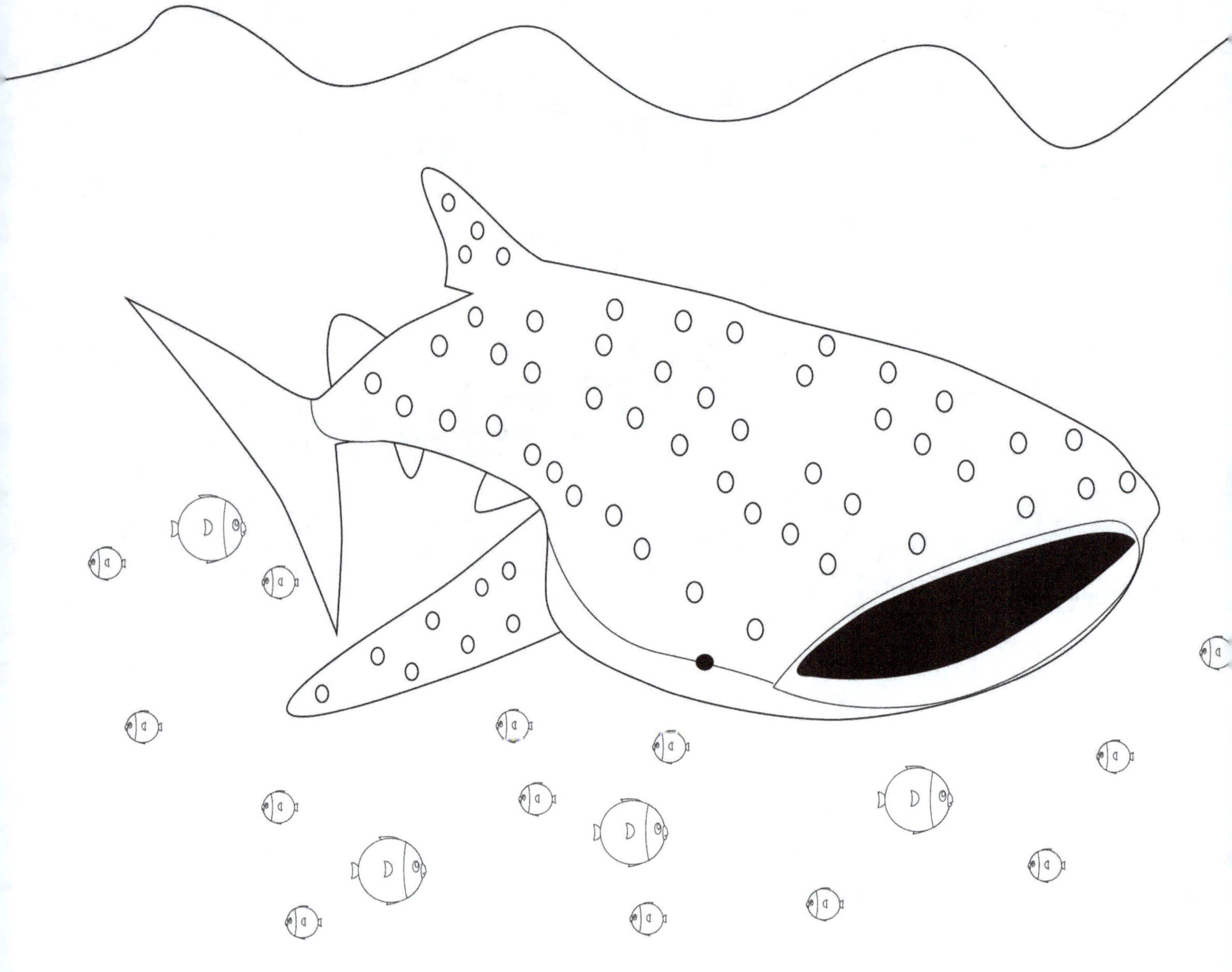

Visit us at:

www.adventuresofscubajack.com

www.ingramcontent.com/pod-product-compliance
Lightning Source LLC
Chambersburg PA
CBHW060428010526
44118CB00017B/2410